50 Creative Salad Recipes

By: Kelly Johnson

Table of Contents

- Quinoa and Black Bean Salad
- Watermelon Feta Salad
- Thai Mango Salad
- Mediterranean Chickpea Salad
- Roasted Beet and Goat Cheese Salad
- Caprese Salad with Balsamic Reduction
- Asian Noodle Salad
- Grilled Peach and Arugula Salad
- Spinach and Strawberry Salad
- Greek Orzo Salad
- Cabbage and Apple Slaw
- Pesto Pasta Salad
- Mexican Street Corn Salad
- Lentil and Feta Salad
- Kale and Apple Salad
- Citrus Avocado Salad
- Broccoli and Bacon Salad
- Panzanella (Italian Bread Salad)
- Carrot and Raisin Salad
- Curried Chicken Salad
- Cobb Salad with Avocado Dressing
- Farro and Roasted Vegetable Salad
- Mediterranean Couscous Salad
- Sweet Potato and Black Bean Salad
- Chilled Cucumber and Dill Salad
- Roasted Vegetable Salad with Tahini Dressing
- Spinach, Bacon, and Egg Salad
- Greek Salad with Quinoa
- Edamame and Corn Salad
- Thai Peanut Crunch Salad
- Fruit and Nut Salad with Honey Vinaigrette
- Zucchini Noodle Salad
- Caprese Pasta Salad
- Curried Quinoa and Raisin Salad
- Chopped Salad with Lemon Vinaigrette
- Avocado and Tomato Salad

- Grilled Vegetable Salad with Feta
- Asian Slaw with Sesame Dressing
- Roasted Chickpea Salad
- Arugula and Pear Salad with Walnuts
- Caesar Salad with Grilled Shrimp
- Fennel and Citrus Salad
- Thai Basil Chicken Salad
- Burrata and Tomato Salad
- Roasted Garlic and Cauliflower Salad
- Spicy Chickpea and Kale Salad
- Beet and Orange Salad
- Cucumber and Tomato Salad with Feta
- Spinach and Lentil Salad
- Barley Salad with Herbs and Lemon

Quinoa and Black Bean Salad

Ingredients:

- **1 cup** quinoa, rinsed
- **2 cups** water
- **1 can (15 oz)** black beans, drained and rinsed
- **1 cup** cherry tomatoes, halved
- **1/2 cup** corn kernels (fresh, frozen, or canned)
- **1/4 cup** red onion, finely chopped
- **1/4 cup** fresh cilantro, chopped
- **1 avocado**, diced (optional)

Dressing:

- **1/4 cup** olive oil
- **2 tbsp** lime juice (about 1 lime)
- **1 tsp** ground cumin
- **1 clove** garlic, minced
- **Salt and pepper** to taste

Instructions:

1. **Cook the quinoa:** In a pot, combine the quinoa and water. Bring to a boil, then reduce heat to low, cover, and simmer for 15 minutes until water is absorbed. Fluff with a fork and let cool.
2. **Prepare the dressing:** In a small bowl, whisk together olive oil, lime juice, cumin, garlic, salt, and pepper.
3. **Assemble the salad:** In a large bowl, combine cooked quinoa, black beans, tomatoes, corn, red onion, and cilantro. Add the diced avocado if using.
4. **Add the dressing:** Pour the dressing over the salad and toss until everything is well-coated.
5. **Chill and serve:** For best flavor, refrigerate for 20-30 minutes before serving. Enjoy cold or at room temperature!

Watermelon Feta Salad

Ingredients:

- **4 cups** watermelon, cubed
- **1/2 cup** feta cheese, crumbled
- **1/4 cup** fresh mint leaves, chopped
- **2 tbsp** olive oil
- **1 tbsp** lime juice
- **Salt and pepper** to taste

Instructions:

1. Combine watermelon, feta, and mint in a large bowl.
2. Drizzle with olive oil and lime juice.
3. Season with salt and pepper, toss gently, and serve chilled.

Thai Mango Salad

Ingredients:

- **2 ripe mangoes**, julienned
- **1/2 cucumber**, sliced
- **1/4 cup** red bell pepper, thinly sliced
- **1/4 cup** red onion, thinly sliced
- **1/4 cup** fresh cilantro, chopped
- **2 tbsp** peanuts, crushed

Dressing:

- **2 tbsp** lime juice
- **1 tbsp** fish sauce or soy sauce
- **1 tsp** sugar
- **1 tsp** chili flakes

Instructions:

1. Combine mango, cucumber, bell pepper, onion, and cilantro.
2. Whisk together the dressing and pour over the salad.
3. Toss well and top with crushed peanuts.

Mediterranean Chickpea Salad

Ingredients:

- **1 can (15 oz)** chickpeas, drained and rinsed
- **1/2 cucumber**, chopped
- **1 cup** cherry tomatoes, halved
- **1/4 cup** red onion, finely sliced
- **1/4 cup** feta cheese, crumbled
- **2 tbsp** fresh parsley, chopped

Dressing:

- **3 tbsp** olive oil
- **1 tbsp** lemon juice
- **1 tsp** oregano
- **Salt and pepper** to taste

Instructions:

1. In a large bowl, combine chickpeas, cucumber, tomatoes, onion, and feta.
2. Whisk together dressing ingredients and pour over the salad.
3. Toss gently and garnish with parsley.

Roasted Beet and Goat Cheese Salad

Ingredients:

- **4 beets**, roasted and sliced
- **1/4 cup** goat cheese, crumbled
- **1/4 cup** walnuts, toasted
- **2 cups** mixed greens
- **2 tbsp** balsamic glaze

Instructions:

1. Arrange greens on a plate and top with roasted beets, goat cheese, and walnuts.
2. Drizzle with balsamic glaze before serving.

Caprese Salad with Balsamic Reduction

Ingredients:

- **3 large tomatoes**, sliced
- **1 ball (8 oz)** fresh mozzarella, sliced
- **1/4 cup** fresh basil leaves
- **2 tbsp** olive oil
- **1/4 cup** balsamic reduction

Instructions:

1. Arrange tomato and mozzarella slices alternately on a platter.
2. Tuck basil leaves between the layers.
3. Drizzle with olive oil and balsamic reduction.

Asian Noodle Salad

Ingredients:

- **8 oz** rice noodles, cooked
- **1/2 red bell pepper**, sliced
- **1/4 cup** shredded carrots
- **1/4 cup** cucumber, julienned
- **2 tbsp** sesame seeds
- **2 tbsp** chopped green onions

Dressing:

- **3 tbsp** soy sauce
- **2 tbsp** sesame oil
- **1 tbsp** rice vinegar
- **1 tsp** honey

Instructions:

1. Combine cooked noodles, bell pepper, carrots, cucumber, and green onions.
2. Whisk together dressing ingredients and pour over the noodles.
3. Toss well and sprinkle with sesame seeds.

Grilled Peach and Arugula Salad

Ingredients:

- **2 peaches**, halved and grilled
- **2 cups** arugula
- **1/4 cup** goat cheese, crumbled
- **1/4 cup** pecans, toasted
- **2 tbsp** balsamic glaze

Instructions:

1. Arrange arugula on a plate.
2. Top with grilled peach slices, goat cheese, and pecans.
3. Drizzle with balsamic glaze before serving.

Spinach and Strawberry Salad

Ingredients:

- 4 cups fresh spinach
- 1 cup strawberries, sliced
- ¼ cup sliced almonds
- ¼ cup feta cheese, crumbled
- 2 tablespoons balsamic vinaigrette

Instructions:

1. **Combine**: In a large bowl, combine spinach, strawberries, almonds, and feta.
2. **Dress**: Drizzle with balsamic vinaigrette and toss gently before serving.

Greek Orzo Salad

Ingredients:

- 1 cup cooked orzo pasta
- 1 cup cherry tomatoes, halved
- ½ cup cucumber, diced
- ¼ cup red onion, finely chopped
- ½ cup Kalamata olives, pitted and sliced
- ¼ cup feta cheese, crumbled
- 2 tablespoons olive oil
- 1 tablespoon red wine vinegar
- Salt and pepper to taste

Instructions:

1. **Mix**: In a large bowl, combine orzo, tomatoes, cucumber, onion, olives, and feta.
2. **Dress**: In a small bowl, whisk together olive oil, vinegar, salt, and pepper. Pour over salad and toss to combine.

Cabbage and Apple Slaw

Ingredients:

- 4 cups green cabbage, shredded
- 1 cup red cabbage, shredded
- 1 apple, cored and thinly sliced
- ¼ cup carrots, grated
- ¼ cup mayonnaise
- 1 tablespoon apple cider vinegar
- Salt and pepper to taste

Instructions:

1. **Combine**: In a large bowl, mix cabbage, apple, and carrots.
2. **Dress**: In a small bowl, whisk together mayonnaise, vinegar, salt, and pepper. Pour over slaw and toss to combine.

Pesto Pasta Salad

Ingredients:

- 2 cups cooked pasta (your choice)
- ½ cup pesto
- 1 cup cherry tomatoes, halved
- ½ cup mozzarella balls, halved
- ¼ cup pine nuts, toasted

Instructions:

1. **Combine**: In a large bowl, mix pasta, pesto, tomatoes, mozzarella, and pine nuts.
2. **Serve**: Toss gently and serve chilled or at room temperature.

Mexican Street Corn Salad

Ingredients:

- 4 ears corn, grilled and kernels removed
- ½ cup mayonnaise
- 1 tablespoon lime juice
- 1 teaspoon chili powder
- ¼ cup cotija cheese, crumbled
- ¼ cup cilantro, chopped

Instructions:

1. **Combine**: In a large bowl, mix corn, mayonnaise, lime juice, chili powder, cotija, and cilantro.
2. **Serve**: Toss to combine and serve chilled.

Lentil and Feta Salad

Ingredients:

- 2 cups cooked lentils
- 1 cup cherry tomatoes, halved
- ½ cup cucumber, diced
- ¼ cup red onion, finely chopped
- ½ cup feta cheese, crumbled
- 2 tablespoons olive oil
- 1 tablespoon lemon juice
- Salt and pepper to taste

Instructions:

1. **Combine**: In a large bowl, mix lentils, tomatoes, cucumber, onion, and feta.
2. **Dress**: Drizzle with olive oil, lemon juice, salt, and pepper. Toss to combine.

Kale and Apple Salad

Ingredients:

- 4 cups kale, chopped
- 1 apple, cored and thinly sliced
- ¼ cup walnuts, toasted
- ¼ cup feta cheese, crumbled
- 2 tablespoons balsamic vinaigrette

Instructions:

1. **Combine**: In a large bowl, mix kale, apple, walnuts, and feta.
2. **Dress**: Drizzle with balsamic vinaigrette and toss gently before serving.

Citrus Avocado Salad

Ingredients:

- 2 oranges, peeled and segmented
- 1 avocado, diced
- ¼ red onion, thinly sliced
- 2 cups mixed greens
- 2 tablespoons olive oil
- 1 tablespoon lime juice
- Salt and pepper to taste

Instructions:

1. **Combine**: In a large bowl, mix oranges, avocado, red onion, and mixed greens.
2. **Dress**: Drizzle with olive oil, lime juice, salt, and pepper. Toss to combine.

Broccoli and Bacon Salad

Ingredients:

- 4 cups broccoli florets
- 6 strips bacon, cooked and crumbled
- ½ cup red onion, finely chopped
- ½ cup shredded cheddar cheese
- ¼ cup sunflower seeds
- ½ cup mayonnaise
- 2 tablespoons apple cider vinegar
- Salt and pepper to taste

Instructions:

1. **Combine**: In a large bowl, mix broccoli, bacon, onion, cheese, and sunflower seeds.
2. **Dress**: In a small bowl, whisk together mayonnaise, vinegar, salt, and pepper. Pour over salad and toss to combine.

Panzanella (Italian Bread Salad)

Ingredients:

- 4 cups day-old crusty bread, cubed
- 2 cups ripe tomatoes, diced
- 1 cucumber, diced
- ½ red onion, thinly sliced
- ¼ cup fresh basil leaves, torn
- ¼ cup olive oil
- 2 tablespoons red wine vinegar
- Salt and pepper to taste

Instructions:

1. **Combine**: In a large bowl, mix bread, tomatoes, cucumber, onion, and basil.
2. **Dress**: Drizzle with olive oil, vinegar, salt, and pepper. Toss to combine and let sit for 30 minutes before serving.

Carrot and Raisin Salad

Ingredients:

- 4 cups grated carrots
- 1 cup raisins
- ½ cup mayonnaise
- 2 tablespoons honey
- 1 tablespoon lemon juice
- Salt and pepper to taste

Instructions:

1. **Combine**: In a large bowl, mix grated carrots and raisins.
2. **Dress**: In a small bowl, whisk together mayonnaise, honey, lemon juice, salt, and pepper. Pour over carrot mixture and toss to combine.

Curried Chicken Salad

Ingredients:

- 2 cups cooked chicken, diced
- 1 cup celery, chopped
- ½ cup grapes, halved
- ¼ cup slivered almonds
- ¼ cup mayonnaise
- 1 tablespoon curry powder
- Salt and pepper to taste

Instructions:

1. **Combine**: In a large bowl, mix chicken, celery, grapes, and almonds.
2. **Dress**: In a small bowl, whisk together mayonnaise, curry powder, salt, and pepper. Pour over salad and toss to combine.

Cobb Salad with Avocado Dressing

Ingredients:

- 4 cups mixed greens
- 1 cup cooked chicken, diced
- ½ cup bacon, cooked and crumbled
- ½ cup cherry tomatoes, halved
- ¼ cup blue cheese, crumbled
- 2 hard-boiled eggs, chopped
- 1 avocado
- 2 tablespoons lime juice
- Salt and pepper to taste

Instructions:

1. **Make Dressing**: In a blender, combine avocado, lime juice, salt, and pepper. Blend until smooth.
2. **Combine**: In a large bowl, layer greens, chicken, bacon, tomatoes, blue cheese, and eggs. Drizzle with avocado dressing before serving.

Farro and Roasted Vegetable Salad

Ingredients:

- 1 cup cooked farro
- 2 cups assorted roasted vegetables (zucchini, bell peppers, carrots)
- ½ cup cherry tomatoes, halved
- ¼ cup feta cheese, crumbled
- 2 tablespoons olive oil
- 1 tablespoon balsamic vinegar
- Salt and pepper to taste

Instructions:

1. **Combine**: In a large bowl, mix farro, roasted vegetables, tomatoes, and feta.
2. **Dress**: Drizzle with olive oil, balsamic vinegar, salt, and pepper. Toss to combine.

Mediterranean Couscous Salad

Ingredients:

- 1 cup cooked couscous
- 1 cup cherry tomatoes, halved
- ½ cucumber, diced
- ¼ cup Kalamata olives, pitted and sliced
- ½ cup feta cheese, crumbled
- 2 tablespoons olive oil
- 1 tablespoon lemon juice
- Salt and pepper to taste

Instructions:

1. **Combine**: In a large bowl, mix couscous, tomatoes, cucumber, olives, and feta.
2. **Dress**: Drizzle with olive oil, lemon juice, salt, and pepper. Toss to combine.

Sweet Potato and Black Bean Salad

Ingredients:

- 2 cups roasted sweet potatoes, cubed
- 1 can black beans, drained and rinsed
- 1 red bell pepper, diced
- ¼ cup red onion, finely chopped
- ¼ cup cilantro, chopped
- 2 tablespoons lime juice
- Salt and pepper to taste

Instructions:

1. **Combine**: In a large bowl, mix sweet potatoes, black beans, bell pepper, onion, and cilantro.
2. **Dress**: Drizzle with lime juice, salt, and pepper. Toss to combine and serve.

Chilled Cucumber and Dill Salad

Ingredients:

- 4 cups cucumber, thinly sliced
- ½ cup Greek yogurt
- 2 tablespoons fresh dill, chopped
- 1 tablespoon lemon juice
- Salt and pepper to taste

Instructions:

1. **Combine**: In a large bowl, mix cucumbers, yogurt, dill, lemon juice, salt, and pepper.
2. **Chill**: Refrigerate for at least 30 minutes before serving to enhance flavors.

Roasted Vegetable Salad with Tahini Dressing

Ingredients:

- 2 cups assorted roasted vegetables (bell peppers, zucchini, carrots)
- 1 cup arugula or mixed greens
- ¼ cup tahini
- 2 tablespoons lemon juice
- 1 tablespoon maple syrup
- Salt and pepper to taste

Instructions:

1. **Make Dressing**: In a small bowl, whisk tahini, lemon juice, maple syrup, salt, and pepper until smooth.
2. **Combine**: In a large bowl, mix roasted vegetables and greens. Drizzle with tahini dressing before serving.

Spinach, Bacon, and Egg Salad

Ingredients:

- 4 cups fresh spinach
- 4 strips bacon, cooked and crumbled
- 2 hard-boiled eggs, sliced
- ½ cup cherry tomatoes, halved
- ¼ cup red onion, thinly sliced
- ¼ cup balsamic vinaigrette

Instructions:

1. **Combine**: In a large bowl, mix spinach, bacon, eggs, tomatoes, and onion.
2. **Dress**: Drizzle with balsamic vinaigrette and toss to combine.

Greek Salad with Quinoa

Ingredients:

- 1 cup cooked quinoa
- 2 cups cherry tomatoes, halved
- 1 cucumber, diced
- ½ cup red onion, diced
- ½ cup Kalamata olives, pitted and halved
- ¼ cup feta cheese, crumbled
- 2 tablespoons olive oil
- 1 tablespoon red wine vinegar
- Salt and pepper to taste

Instructions:

1. **Combine**: In a large bowl, mix quinoa, tomatoes, cucumber, onion, olives, and feta.
2. **Dress**: Drizzle with olive oil, vinegar, salt, and pepper. Toss to combine.

Edamame and Corn Salad

Ingredients:

- 1 cup edamame, shelled and cooked
- 1 cup corn (fresh or frozen)
- ½ red bell pepper, diced
- ¼ cup green onions, chopped
- 2 tablespoons lime juice
- Salt and pepper to taste

Instructions:

1. **Combine**: In a large bowl, mix edamame, corn, bell pepper, and green onions.
2. **Dress**: Drizzle with lime juice, salt, and pepper. Toss to combine.

Thai Peanut Crunch Salad

Ingredients:

- 4 cups mixed greens
- 1 cup shredded carrots
- 1 cup red cabbage, shredded
- ½ cup edamame, shelled
- ¼ cup chopped peanuts
- ¼ cup cilantro, chopped
- ¼ cup peanut butter
- 2 tablespoons soy sauce
- 1 tablespoon lime juice
- 1 tablespoon honey

Instructions:

1. **Make Dressing**: In a small bowl, whisk together peanut butter, soy sauce, lime juice, and honey until smooth.
2. **Combine**: In a large bowl, mix greens, carrots, cabbage, edamame, peanuts, and cilantro. Drizzle with dressing before serving.

Fruit and Nut Salad with Honey Vinaigrette

Ingredients:

- 4 cups mixed greens
- 1 cup mixed fresh fruit (berries, apple slices, oranges)
- ½ cup nuts (walnuts, pecans, or almonds)
- ¼ cup feta cheese, crumbled
- 2 tablespoons honey
- 1 tablespoon apple cider vinegar
- Salt and pepper to taste

Instructions:

1. **Make Dressing**: In a small bowl, whisk honey, vinegar, salt, and pepper until well combined.
2. **Combine**: In a large bowl, mix greens, fruit, nuts, and feta. Drizzle with honey vinaigrette before serving.

Zucchini Noodle Salad

Ingredients:

- 4 cups zucchini noodles (spiralized)
- 1 cup cherry tomatoes, halved
- ½ cup bell pepper, diced
- ¼ cup red onion, thinly sliced
- 2 tablespoons olive oil
- 1 tablespoon balsamic vinegar
- Salt and pepper to taste

Instructions:

1. **Combine**: In a large bowl, mix zucchini noodles, tomatoes, bell pepper, and onion.
2. **Dress**: Drizzle with olive oil, balsamic vinegar, salt, and pepper. Toss to combine and serve immediately.

Caprese Pasta Salad

Ingredients:

- 8 ounces pasta (fusilli or penne)
- 1 cup cherry tomatoes, halved
- 1 cup mozzarella balls, halved
- ½ cup fresh basil leaves, torn
- ¼ cup olive oil
- 2 tablespoons balsamic vinegar
- Salt and pepper to taste

Instructions:

1. **Cook Pasta**: Cook pasta according to package instructions; drain and cool.
2. **Combine**: In a large bowl, mix pasta, tomatoes, mozzarella, and basil.
3. **Dress**: Drizzle with olive oil, balsamic vinegar, salt, and pepper. Toss to combine.

Curried Quinoa and Raisin Salad

Ingredients:

- 1 cup cooked quinoa
- ½ cup raisins
- ½ cup diced bell peppers
- ¼ cup chopped green onions
- ¼ cup chopped cilantro
- 2 tablespoons olive oil
- 1 tablespoon curry powder
- Salt and pepper to taste

Instructions:

1. **Combine**: In a large bowl, mix quinoa, raisins, bell peppers, green onions, and cilantro.
2. **Dress**: Drizzle with olive oil, sprinkle curry powder, salt, and pepper. Toss to combine.

Chopped Salad with Lemon Vinaigrette

Ingredients:

- 2 cups romaine lettuce, chopped
- 1 cup cucumber, diced
- 1 cup cherry tomatoes, halved
- ½ cup red onion, diced
- ½ cup bell pepper, diced
- ¼ cup olive oil
- 2 tablespoons lemon juice
- Salt and pepper to taste

Instructions:

1. **Combine**: In a large bowl, mix lettuce, cucumber, tomatoes, onion, and bell pepper.
2. **Dress**: Whisk together olive oil, lemon juice, salt, and pepper. Drizzle over salad and toss to combine.

Avocado and Tomato Salad

Ingredients:

- 2 ripe avocados, diced
- 2 cups cherry tomatoes, halved
- ¼ cup red onion, finely chopped
- ¼ cup fresh cilantro, chopped
- 2 tablespoons lime juice
- Salt and pepper to taste

Instructions:

1. **Combine**: In a large bowl, mix avocados, tomatoes, onion, and cilantro.
2. **Dress**: Drizzle with lime juice, salt, and pepper. Toss gently to combine.

Grilled Vegetable Salad with Feta

Ingredients:

- 2 cups assorted grilled vegetables (zucchini, bell peppers, eggplant)
- 4 cups mixed greens
- ½ cup feta cheese, crumbled
- ¼ cup balsamic glaze
- Salt and pepper to taste

Instructions:

1. **Combine**: In a large bowl, mix grilled vegetables and greens.
2. **Dress**: Drizzle with balsamic glaze, sprinkle feta, salt, and pepper. Toss gently to combine.

Asian Slaw with Sesame Dressing

Ingredients:

- 4 cups shredded cabbage (green and purple)
- 1 cup shredded carrots
- ½ cup sliced green onions
- ¼ cup sesame seeds
- ¼ cup rice vinegar
- 2 tablespoons soy sauce
- 1 tablespoon sesame oil
- 1 tablespoon honey

Instructions:

1. **Make Dressing**: In a small bowl, whisk together vinegar, soy sauce, sesame oil, and honey.
2. **Combine**: In a large bowl, mix cabbage, carrots, green onions, and sesame seeds. Drizzle with dressing and toss to combine.

Roasted Chickpea Salad

Ingredients:

- 1 can (15 oz) chickpeas, drained and rinsed
- 1 teaspoon olive oil
- 1 teaspoon smoked paprika
- 4 cups mixed greens
- ½ cup cherry tomatoes, halved
- ¼ cup cucumber, diced
- 2 tablespoons tahini dressing

Instructions:

1. **Roast Chickpeas**: Preheat oven to 400°F (200°C). Toss chickpeas with olive oil and paprika, spread on a baking sheet, and roast for 20-25 minutes until crispy.
2. **Combine**: In a large bowl, mix greens, tomatoes, cucumber, and roasted chickpeas. Drizzle with tahini dressing and toss to combine.

Arugula and Pear Salad with Walnuts

Ingredients:

- 4 cups arugula
- 1 ripe pear, thinly sliced
- ½ cup walnuts, toasted
- ¼ cup crumbled blue cheese
- 2 tablespoons olive oil
- 1 tablespoon balsamic vinegar
- Salt and pepper to taste

Instructions:

1. **Combine**: In a large bowl, mix arugula, pear, walnuts, and blue cheese.
2. **Dress**: Drizzle with olive oil, balsamic vinegar, salt, and pepper. Toss gently to combine.

Caesar Salad with Grilled Shrimp

Ingredients:

- 1 lb shrimp, peeled and deveined
- 4 cups romaine lettuce, chopped
- ½ cup Caesar dressing
- ¼ cup grated Parmesan cheese
- Croutons for topping
- Salt and pepper to taste
- Olive oil for grilling

Instructions:

1. **Grill Shrimp**: Preheat grill to medium-high. Toss shrimp with olive oil, salt, and pepper. Grill for 2-3 minutes on each side until cooked.
2. **Combine**: In a large bowl, mix lettuce with Caesar dressing.
3. **Serve**: Top with grilled shrimp, Parmesan cheese, and croutons.

Fennel and Citrus Salad

Ingredients:

- 1 bulb fennel, thinly sliced
- 2 oranges, segmented
- 1 grapefruit, segmented
- ¼ cup red onion, thinly sliced
- ¼ cup olive oil
- 2 tablespoons white wine vinegar
- Salt and pepper to taste
- Fresh dill for garnish

Instructions:

1. **Combine**: In a large bowl, mix fennel, orange segments, grapefruit segments, and red onion.
2. **Dress**: Whisk together olive oil, vinegar, salt, and pepper; drizzle over salad and toss gently.
3. **Garnish**: Top with fresh dill before serving.

Thai Basil Chicken Salad

Ingredients:

- 1 lb ground chicken
- 2 cups mixed greens
- 1 cup shredded carrots
- ½ cup red bell pepper, thinly sliced
- ¼ cup fresh Thai basil leaves
- 2 tablespoons soy sauce
- 1 tablespoon lime juice
- 1 teaspoon sesame oil

Instructions:

1. **Cook Chicken**: In a skillet, cook ground chicken over medium heat until browned; add soy sauce, lime juice, and sesame oil.
2. **Combine**: In a large bowl, mix greens, carrots, bell pepper, and basil.
3. **Serve**: Top with cooked chicken and toss to combine.

Burrata and Tomato Salad

Ingredients:

- 1 ball burrata cheese
- 2 cups heirloom tomatoes, sliced
- ¼ cup fresh basil leaves
- 2 tablespoons olive oil
- 1 tablespoon balsamic glaze
- Salt and pepper to taste

Instructions:

1. **Assemble**: On a serving platter, arrange tomato slices and burrata.
2. **Dress**: Drizzle with olive oil and balsamic glaze; sprinkle with salt and pepper.
3. **Garnish**: Top with fresh basil leaves before serving.

Roasted Garlic and Cauliflower Salad

Ingredients:

- 1 head cauliflower, cut into florets
- 4 cloves garlic, minced
- ¼ cup olive oil
- 2 tablespoons lemon juice
- ½ cup parsley, chopped
- Salt and pepper to taste

Instructions:

1. **Roast Cauliflower**: Preheat oven to 425°F (220°C). Toss cauliflower with garlic, olive oil, salt, and pepper; roast for 25-30 minutes until golden.
2. **Combine**: In a large bowl, mix roasted cauliflower with lemon juice and parsley.
3. **Serve**: Toss gently before serving.

Spicy Chickpea and Kale Salad

Ingredients:

- 1 can (15 oz) chickpeas, drained and rinsed
- 4 cups kale, chopped
- ½ cup cherry tomatoes, halved
- ¼ cup red onion, thinly sliced
- 2 tablespoons olive oil
- 1 teaspoon chili flakes
- Salt and pepper to taste

Instructions:

1. **Roast Chickpeas**: Preheat oven to 400°F (200°C). Toss chickpeas with olive oil, chili flakes, salt, and pepper; roast for 20-25 minutes until crispy.
2. **Combine**: In a large bowl, mix kale, tomatoes, and red onion.
3. **Serve**: Top with roasted chickpeas and toss to combine.

Beet and Orange Salad

Ingredients:

- 2 cups cooked beets, sliced
- 2 oranges, segmented
- ¼ cup goat cheese, crumbled
- ¼ cup walnuts, toasted
- 2 tablespoons olive oil
- Salt and pepper to taste

Instructions:

1. **Combine**: In a large bowl, mix beets, orange segments, goat cheese, and walnuts.
2. **Dress**: Drizzle with olive oil, salt, and pepper; toss gently to combine.
3. **Serve**: Arrange on a platter before serving.

Cucumber and Tomato Salad with Feta

Ingredients:

- 2 cups cucumber, diced
- 2 cups cherry tomatoes, halved
- ½ cup feta cheese, crumbled
- ¼ cup red onion, thinly sliced
- 2 tablespoons olive oil
- 1 tablespoon red wine vinegar
- Salt and pepper to taste

Instructions:

1. **Combine**: In a large bowl, mix cucumber, tomatoes, feta, and red onion.
2. **Dress**: Drizzle with olive oil, vinegar, salt, and pepper. Toss gently to combine.
3. **Serve**: Enjoy chilled.

Spinach and Lentil Salad

Ingredients:

- 2 cups fresh spinach, chopped
- 1 cup cooked lentils
- ½ red onion, thinly sliced
- 1 cup cherry tomatoes, halved
- ¼ cup feta cheese, crumbled
- ¼ cup walnuts, chopped
- 3 tablespoons olive oil
- 1 tablespoon red wine vinegar
- Salt and pepper to taste

Instructions:

1. **Combine**: In a large bowl, mix spinach, lentils, red onion, cherry tomatoes, feta cheese, and walnuts.
2. **Dress**: In a small bowl, whisk together olive oil, vinegar, salt, and pepper.
3. **Serve**: Drizzle the dressing over the salad, toss gently, and serve immediately.

Barley Salad with Herbs and Lemon

Ingredients:

- 1 cup barley, cooked and cooled
- 1 cup cucumber, diced
- ½ cup bell pepper, diced
- ½ cup cherry tomatoes, halved
- ¼ cup fresh parsley, chopped
- ¼ cup fresh mint, chopped
- 2 tablespoons olive oil
- Juice of 1 lemon
- Salt and pepper to taste

Instructions:

1. **Combine**: In a large bowl, mix cooked barley, cucumber, bell pepper, cherry tomatoes, parsley, and mint.
2. **Dress**: In a small bowl, whisk together olive oil, lemon juice, salt, and pepper.
3. **Serve**: Pour the dressing over the salad, toss well, and serve chilled or at room temperature.

www.ingramcontent.com/pod-product-compliance
Lightning Source LLC
LaVergne TN
LVHW081334060526
838201LV00055B/2649